CONTEMPLATIONS ON GOD AND ORGASM
REVISED EDITION

CATHERINE FAIRFIELD HAYES

authorHOUSE®

AuthorHouse™
1663 Liberty Drive
Bloomington, IN 47403
www.authorhouse.com
Phone: 833-262-8899

Previously Published by Lynn Brown & Associates

Published by AuthorHouse 03/17/2021

ISBN: 978-1-7283-1457-0 (sc)
ISBN: 978-1-7283-1456-3 (e)

Print information available on the last page.

Introduction

If the Three Wise Men were alive today—i.e., Balthasar, Melchior and Gaspar, the Magi who followed the star of Bethlehem to the manger where Jesus was born—they would most likely be in jail. It would not be for spreading any false propaganda about the birth of Jesus, but for the crime of incest.

As members of the priestly class of Persia, the Magi, they were practitioners of *Khvetukdas*—i.e., next-of-kin marriage—whose tenets were as follows:

> "The consummation of the mutual assistance of men is *Khvetukdas*...That union...is...that with nearest kinsfolk, and, among near kinsfolk, that with those next-of-kin; and the mutual connection of the three kinds of nearest kin, which are father and daughter, son and she who bore him, and brother and sister...is the most complete that I have considered."*

(Thus explained by a Zoroastrian priest to a Jewish objector.)* Others who doubted might have reconsidered its merits by this efficacious description:

> "When the millenium is about to dawn, 'all mankind will perform *Khvetukdas*, and every fiend will perish through the miracle of *Khvetukdas*. The first time that a man practices it a thousand demons will die, and two thousand wizards and witches...and when he goes near it four times, it is known that a man and a woman become perfect...Whoever keeps one year in a marriage of *Khvetukdas* becomes just as though one-third of all this world...had been given by him...unto a righteous man...And when he keeps four years in

his marriage, and his (funeral) ritual is performed, it is known that his soul goes into the supreme heaven; and when the ritual is not performed, it goes thereby to the ordinary heaven. The good deeds of those who observe *Khvetukdas* are a hundred times more effacacious than the same deeds performed by other pious men; and the penalty for dissuading from it is hell." *

Since this practice was well known throughout the classical world, and by no means pleasing to everyone, why had the early Christian fathers brought the Magi into the manger? Could the answer have come in the 19th century, when the Crucifixion was interpreted in psychoanalytical terms as a symbol of incest?

"Look upon the cross, with its outspread arms, and you will agree with me. The Son of God hangs and dies upon it. The Kreuz (cross, os sacrum) is the mother, and upon the mother we all of us must die. Oedipus! Oedipus!**

But other religions have also connected man's sexual desires to God. In Judaism, the Divine Covenant between God and man is circumcision:

"And God said to Abraham...This is my covenant which you shall keep...Every male among you shall be circumcised...in the flesh of your foreskins...So shall my covenant be in your flesh an everlasting covenant." (Genesis 17)

In ancient Egypt, the word of God was symbolized by the phallus of Osiris, and in the Old and New Testament the word of God is repeatedly used. The famous opening of John is thus:

* Encyclopedia of Religion and Ethics, L.H. Gray, ed. By James Hastings, pgs. 457-458.
** The Book of the It," Georg Groddeck, The New American Library, 1961, p. 115, paperback.

"In the beginning was the Word, and the Word was with God, and the Word was God."

If "in the beginning" refers to the creation of human life, how can it happen without the male organ—i.e., the Word? Is this why God is a "Him," because he speaks through the penis?

Before there were laws, before there was written history, before God said "Let there be light," and created man in his own image, there was Deep Time (a period roughly 50,000, 500,000, even 2.6 million years ago) and a world "without form and void" inhabited by unruly hominds. What better way to reign them in than to turn orgasm into a living spirit, and later, the living spirit of God, as they evolved into us? Wouldn't that make any man afraid of his own shadow?

What is truth? Can we separate God from orgasm if He is it and it is us?

Preface

Perhaps the real impetus for writing this book has come about from the many times that, after a fantastic climax, God's presence becomes part of the mix. His name rushes to my lips—me, an unbeliever. I call to Him, I call Him to me, He is so much a part of it, a part of the climax. Indeed, He *is* the climax, and to Him I give thanks—me, I repeat, an unbeliever. But in that moment of ecstasy, I *do* believe: I can no more deny the reality of the orgasm than I can deny the reality of His existence.

From this experience, this awareness of my inability to separate the Supreme Being from the Supreme Moment, I've come to believe that God and orgasm are two faces of the same coin. But this realization didn't come overnight. In fact, it took several years to evolve, and may not have evolved at all had I not heard a scholar discussing the peculiar doctrine of Khvetukdas and its adherents, the Magi, on the radio. I was intrigued at once. The Magi? The three Wise Men from the East who followed the star to Bethlehem, and to the manger where Jesus was born? Really?

What child doesn't know the story? Or seen a Nativity somewhere— under a Christmas tree or in a department store: Mary and Joseph and the baby Jesus, the kneeling shepherds, the grazing animals and, of course, the three Magi—sometimes called the Three Kings— bearing gifts of gold, frankincense and myrrh. It is such a beautiful scene, and so powerful; it's indelible impression leaves one marked for life.

The news, I confess, shocked me—or better yet, mesmerized me? Or how about titillated?

Whatever it was, I had to learn more. Whether or not I was motivated by my own Freudian desires and childhood orgasms, Khvetukdas beckoned. So, like the three Wise Men following the star, I entered the unknown desert of this ancient world in search of the answer: why, with their unpalatable idea that the penalty for

dissuading from Khvetukdas was hell, were the Magi in the manger, in the first place?

(◊)

"Magic, a ritual performance or activity believed to influence human or natural events through access to the external mystical force* beyond the ordinary human sphere. It is the core of many religious systems and central in most preliterate cultures. At one time magic was considered entirely distinct from religion, as consisting of external manipulations rather than supplication and inner grace, and is still so considered by many religious thinkers. Contemporary anthropologists and historians of religion, however, tend to hold that since both magic and religion are concerned with the effects on human existence of outside mystical forces,* they are generically and similar and connected."**

Examples of this connection aren't hard to find. There is Mithras, for instance, the Zoroastrian god of light; when he slays the sacred bull, wheat and wine spring forth from the bull's body. Now, if his body can be transformed into wheat and wine, and Jesus' body (a millennium later) into wheat (bread) and wine, why cannot orgasm be transformed into God?

And if the ancient Egyptians transformed the phallus of Osiris into the Word, and later, the Gospel of John transformed the Word back into God, then why cannot orgasm also be transformed into God? Does not orgasm come through the penis? Is the origin of His holy name not so much that of a Supreme Being as of the supreme and divine natural force of orgasm—that outside mystical force which has effected human existence, one can surmise, all the way back to the hominids?

> "I will give unto thee the keys to the kingdom of heaven" (Matthew 16:19).

> "The kingdom of God is within you" (Luke 17:21).

---

* Orgasm
** New Encyclopedia Britannica-Micropaedia, Vol. 6, p. 483.

What are these keys? What are these kingdoms? Are the keys magic? Are we in the realm of magical orgasm? Have we sublimated it into Scripture?

This is what I suspect. Whereas other people's scholarship might lead to a Pulitzer Prize or a tenure at Yale, mine has led me to believe that the Magi were right. What they knew was that the way to God— i.e. orgasm—was through sexual union, unpalatable or not. But this being the antithesis of Christianity—didn't Jesus die for our sins?— the Three Kings arrived at the manger to pass the crown down to a new king, basically saying, "yours is the true religion, not ours."

The world still holds tightly to the belief that God exists. How can one say no, if He is, as I believe, in our biology? God has a solid basis—our experience of orgasm. Our mythologies and creation stories, whether they come from the East or the West, are rooted in fertility and procreation. And how does procreation begin but in a blast of supreme, divine, mystical orgasm? Surely this is where He begins, transmogrified through magic eons ago, perhaps from a time when the earth was without form and void, as stated in Genesis: a word which, perhaps not coincidentally, comes from the same Indo-European root as "genitals."

That I was able to write this book, I give all credit to the Magi.

There are many parallels between our experience of God and our experience of orgasm. Since their elusive essence is often expressed by the same words and feelings, could they possibly be two sides of the same coin?

They say there is nothing new under the sun, but perhaps there is, as we contemplate God and orgasm as one.

CONTEMPLATIONS ON GOD AND ORGASM

If our ancestors of bygone times believed in river gods, tree gods and all kind of other gods, why not a god of orgasm? If trees were once believed to be the homes of gods, why couldn't the pelvis (or the human body) be the home of gods who caused humans to desire and love? The home of gods who orchestrated the delicious yet unfathomable (and possibly, in some religions, unutterable) experience we call orgasm?

And if trees were believed to be inhabited by spirits, both good and bad, why couldn't a good spirit—God—and a bad spirit—the Devil—inhabit the pelvis?

&

Does anyone have self-doubt during orgasm? Is there anyone who is not glad to be alive at that instant? If orgasm can take a person out of his body and every negative feeling he has in it—all the cares, concerns, disappointments, frustration, anger and worry, and if people seek God for the same release and relief of these pressing feelings, could there not be a connection?

&

The word ecstasy (Greek *ekstasis*) means "standing outside oneself." Now, since we know that this is how it feels during that ecstatic moment of orgasm, and since it was the god Dionysus to whom the Greeks credited this wild freedom, who is to say that the concept of orgasmic ecstasy is not paramount to all gods, even the monotheistic god of Western religions?

If a simple kernel of corn can metamorphose into a fluffy treat—popcorn—why can't God be metamorphosed into the ultimate treat—orgasm?

Did the concept of beauty arise from man's desire to catch the elusiveness of orgasm, and make it permanent by such artifices as painting, music and literature? Does our feeling that beauty is real and is a reflection of the universe, stem from the reality of orgasm? Does evil exist because orgasm has been corrupted by too many sexual taboos?

A Christian struggles not to rebel against God, but if God is indeed the transmutation of orgasm, isn't it silly to struggle against Him? To rebel against Mother Nature and the biological sex drive she has installed within us?

Religion teaches us that every power is from God. But if God is orgasm, does it not follow that our concept of power, from friendly persuasion to the deadly force of warfare, originates in the pelvis?

Having just decoded the DNA of gorillas, and discovering that the genes involved in hearing evolved just as rapidly for them as for us, researchers now question the previously-held idea that human language was linked to this genetic change. May I offer the suggestion that the need to control orgasm (hominids gone wild) is what led to the rise of human language?

A team of researchers in France have reported that "when two patients had both hands transplanted, their brains established connections much more quickly with the left hand than the right...though both (patients) had been right-handed before losing their hands."

Is this a sign that the body wishes naturally to be left-handed? And if so, how did most of us come to be right-handed? Paleontological evidence indicates that our hominid ancestors used clubs in the left hand to bash in skulls. Is it too far-fetched to suppose that religion had a hand (no pun intended) in this, teaching (or forcing?) us to be right-handed and, consequently, to be good?

Could levophobia, the fear of objects or events occurring to one's left, have less to do with a universal memory of our murderous hominid ancestors than with that more recent fear of God? And why a baby's right ear reacts faster and more accurately to speech (and eventually to religious edicts) while the left ear prefers music (the dangerous emotional left of the hominids)?

&

Mighty is His name. A perfect rendering for orgasm?

&

And I will give unto thee the keys of the kingdom of heaven. A beautiful metaphor for sexual gratification?

&

If the science is right, does the old saying "cleanliness is next to Godliness" actually mean, keep the genitals clean?

&

A religious person has said that God is there for everyone, and we are all His sons and daughters. Is this not true, in the sense that everyone can climax, and we are all the result?

&

Is orgasm that state of grace in which God shows His loving mercy toward mankind? What can be more lovingly merciful than when wave after wave of glorious orgasm sweeps over us and takes us

3

away (though it be for a brief instant) from all our worries and all our troubles?

(℘)

A Gregorian chant is written in different kinds of scales and cadences than what we are used to, leaving us feeling disoriented and mystical. Now, if liturgical music is meant to emphasize the mystery of faith, then in some way or another does it simulate an intellectual response to orgasm?

(℘)

On viewing the interior diagrams of churches and cathedrals one wonders, are all places of worship but replicas of the womb?

If the structure of a cockroach's brain "is so strangely reminiscent of the human hippocampus," possibly resulting "from a deep and ancient kinship" between us, perhaps we are just as primitively orgasmic.*

(℘)

Is it possible that even the rosary is orgasmic in nature? Why not, if by holding the beads in our hands and reciting its four mysteries—Joyful, Sorrowful, Glorious and Luminous—names which in themselves are expressive of orgasm (Sorrowful being its aftermath when we float back to earth), we feel consoled and closer to God...

---

* Consciousness in a...Cockroach?, Discover Magazine, January 2007

Has anyone ever invoked God's name at the startling onset of orgasm? If so, was this merely a coincidence or does the Subconscious know more than we think?

Religion teaches us that the spirit can free itself from the bonds of flesh. Could that spirit be orgasm?

And if God is, indeed, the metamorphose of orgasm, and the pelvis is the gateway to heaven, then might it not follow that hills and mountains (which mimic the female breast) are also holy and, to the worshiper, the perfect place for the doors of heaven to open?

In Judaism there is a secret word for God. There is also a secret word for life. Since life cannot occur without sex, are the two secrets actually one?

Is the key to religion's mysteries literally within our grasp?

You've heard the expression, "We are all God's children?" Well, if God is the magical emanation of orgasm, and a zygote is the product of orgasm, then no truer words were ever spoken. We *are* all God's children. How can we help it?

The church is a mystic body.

Is it just a coincidence that the Second Coming—the idea that true believers will be transported to heaven at the end of the world— is referred to as the Rapture, a word whose definition (the state of being transported by a lofty emotion such as ecstasy from one place to another, especially to heaven) is such a good parallel to orgasm?

(&

For those who seek "divine reward" on Judgement Day, what could be more divine than an eternity of orgasm? And for those who seek paradise (from the Avestan *pairidaeza*, meaning an enclosure- -*pairi*, about, around, Greek *daeza*, a wall), perhaps it exists not in the sky, but in the vagina. Is not this word for paradise the perfect description?

(&

If God is the mystical emanation of orgasm, and all the world's religions are there as pathways to connect us to God, than is not morality itself an emanation of orgasm?
"I felt (the faith) was the only way to go to heaven."

(&

When a bishop walks down the aisle wearing his golden miter, that suggestive hat with two lips parted invitingly at the top, and sprinkles us with holy water from that extremely suggestive aspergill—a golden rod with a perforated globe on the end— what, one wonders, is it really all about?
Miter: from Mithras, a Persian god worshipped by the Magi.
Magi: priests of ancient Persia noted for their sorcery, hence the word *magic*.

(&

In the Hindu religion, if the many different deities all represent manifestations of the same force, could that force be orgasm?

(&

If orgasm is at the bottom of religion, then would it not follow that all the good which mankind has achieved through religion— compassion, virtue, one's "God-given dignity" and humanity in

general—that all this is but an attribute, a subtle paean to the beauty and majesty of orgasm?

(Q)

When we talk about God's infinite goodness, could we also be talking about the infinite goodness of orgasm? And is it just a coincidence that, in certain church ritual, God's infinite goodness is symbolized by the disbursement of holy water dripped with oil—i.e., symbolic of semen?

(Q)

On the assumption that bipedalism resulted in a physiognomy that resulted in irrepressible orgasm which turned the tide of Nature, then for the answer to the two questions which continue to perplex us: why is our species different from all other species, and by what means has this difference come about—is it toolmaking, language, culture, etc.?—then perhaps the "true believers," those who say we are different "because Homo sapiens possess immortal and God-given souls, chips off the old Divine Block," may have it right after all.

(Q)

If bipedalism led to great sex which led to utter chaos which led to the development (from dire necessity) of a bigger brain which led to thought—i.e., "there is a spirit living in my pelvis" which led to God which led to Civilization (as we know it) which led to what we are today, then the two questions are answered without any great scientific breakthrough because in this case God and Science are one.

(Q)

If a metaphysical source of authority was ultimately responsible for the principles established by the Bill of Rights in 1689, dare we surmise that the very nature of such principles as political freedom, democracy and individual liberty owe their existence to orgasm, if that source of authority should turn out to be the mystical transmutation of God and orgasm?

7

Is there any similarity between God, orgasm and a born-again Christian's desire to be reborn?

If the kingdom of God is within us, and God is our subconscious identity of orgasm, then does the kingdom of God refer to our physical bodies? And if so, could this explain why religion has such a hold on us, because religion *is* us?

Was the creation of language less a product of the mind than a product of our animal instincts? Like an animal smelling with its nose, did words emanate from our physical bodies? Like religion, are words actually *us*?

In God We Trust. (Is there anything more trustworthy than orgasm?)

Is the mystery of faith tied to the mystery of orgasm?

When people's love lives have become too painful to bare, some turn to God—i.e., dedicate their lives to the Church, to a "one-on-one" relationship with God. Is this in order to sublimate orgasm rather than continue to experience it physically? And would this in some way nullify the very concept of celibacy?

Here in Washington D.C. is the Basilica of the National Shrine of the Immaculate Conception—the largest Roman Catholic church in North America. But to the Subconscious mind it is the entrance to the birth canal flanked by a towering penis and a large female breast. Who can question the sanctity of orgasm now, envisioned as such by this impressive formation?

a--penis
b--breast
c--vagina

If, as some scholars contend, the primacy of language rather than politics, war or economics is what fueled the wheels of civilization, and if men came to control orgasm through language, could it be argued that orgasm fueled language, and by extension, civilization itself?

Could natural selection and the evolutionary imperative be nothing more than the desire to experience orgasm, orgasm and more orgasm?

A man in a simple state of mind brought on by Alzheimer's disease, connects music to romance and love. He also connects music to God: "The Lord came to me, made me a holy man, so he gave me these sounds."

Now, if music equals romance and love (i.e., sexual passion), and music equals God, then by deductive thinking, God equals sexual passion (i.e., orgasm). The syllogism appears like this:

If	A (music)	= B (orgasm)
And	A (music)	= C (God)
Then	B (orgasm)	= C (God)

The evangelicals say they are able to communicate with God "on everything from job choice to what shampoo to buy," because "God speaks through the human mind."

Now if God is orgasm, does this mean that orgasm speaks through the human mind? i.e., that our species has sublimated orgasm through words, thoughts, everything we know as culture and civilization? And this is why we speak, to control orgasm?

Unlike Dolly the sheep, Jesus can't be cloned from God because God doesn't have a physical body. Does orgasm?

Were the Dead Sea Scrolls, those ancient parchments documenting the Hebrew Bible—i.e., God, purposefully placed in caves because of their resemblance to the pelvis and the womb?

When Moses asked God what His name was, God said, "I am what I am, I am that I am,"...and orgasm is what it is and never what it isn't.

Since it's only in modern times that science has explained the nature of orgasm, could the enigma or God's name be the enigma

of orgasm? Do these words from the Roman Catholic Church give a hint that this is so?

"In revealing his mysterious name, YHWH.....'I AM WHO I AM,' God says who he and by what name he is to be called. This divine name is mysterious just as God is mystery. It is at once a name revealed and something like the refusal of a name, and hence it better expresses God as what he is—ineffable, and he is the God who makes himself close to men."

Very close, indeed?

(◊

Like a whale's tongue, is God but "a beautiful application of physics...plumbing and heating?"

(◊

Thank God!—i.e., thank orgasm for making us feel good.

(◊

If Paradise is that state of delight to be found in the walled enclosure of the vagina, was Jesus talking about orgasm when he said, in Luke 23, to the condemned man next to him, *"Thou shalt be with me this day in Paradise?"*

(◊

In the Judaic religion, it is prohibited to make an image of God. Since no image of orgasm exists, is this a clue that the two are fundamentally connected?

And if religion has cemented the transportation of God and orgasm, could the idea behind Christianity and its *use* of images be connect to the problem of forbidden Oedipal desires, previously brought forth in classical Greek thought? (The Magi, for instance, were not against incestuous relationships.)

(◊

If orgasm was, indeed, transmogrified into a deity, then it must have occurred in prehistoric times and we will probably never know how it came about; for by the time records began to exist, the idea of deities was already well established.

At that delicious moment when we climax and cry out "Oh my God," is that simply an exclamation of ecstatic emotion, or are we speaking to Him directly (as a child might speak to a favorite toy) and acknowledging that there is indeed a deity living inside the pelvis?

(&

For Franz Kafka and Czeslaw Milosz, "language was a dishonest fabrication, an integral part of the mask that is civilization." Could it be that this dishonest fabrication, this mask has to do with the dishonest fabrication of orgasm into God, which is possibly the basis of language?

If our ancestors in prehistoric times or beyond, in pursuing this ineffable pleasure of orgasm, caused a world of chaos and violence— *In the beginning....the earth was without form and void, and darkness was upon the face of the deep*—then would not the channeling of orgasm through some other medium—say religion, say God—have been a very wise, a very great, a very earth-shattering step in the evolution of our species?

(&

Shakespeare said that all the world's a stage. Could the stage itself be but a replica of the womb?

Perhaps it's only right that we see God as a male figurehead, for if there were no penis to inject into a vagina, how could the Absolute Perfection of orgasm ever take place?

(&

Are the mysteries of aesthetic appeal to be found in the unparalleled beauty of orgasm?

(&

I've just come up with an idea for a new scientific discipline: *Psychotheology*. What amazing truths might come of it, should the underpinnings of theology ever be psychoanalyzed!

(&

"Thanks be to God."
Is there any experience for which we are more thankful than orgasm? And when we say, "Thanks to God..." for this piece of good fortune or that, isn't orgasm the greatest good fortune to come the way of all human beings during the difficult sojourn of life?

(&

Could the worship of orgasm be the biological basis of human social behavior?

(&

I suppose that in the old days, it didn't matter who you had sex with; the whole point was to reach a climax. Is this not as good an explanation as any for natural selection?

(&

If the kingdom of God is, as I suspect, a euphemistic invocation to the sensuous realm of Eros and orgasm, then when Jesus says in John 3, "Unless a man be born again, he cannot see the kingdom of God," what, exactly, are we talking about? Is it, perhaps a nod to Oedipus?

To a son's struggles with all that's forbidden? Is this what makes born again Christianity such a powerful movement, and its adherents so self-righteous?

(◌

If God is rooted in the pelvis, and it's His job to keep the pelvis in line and morality intact, then no wonder that women, being able to orgasm multiple times, aren't ever ordained to be the spokesperson for God. That's just asking for trouble.

(◌

If religion is the sublimation of orgasm, then those men and women who have dedicated themselves to God, such as the clergy, the monks and the nuns, exist in a subliminal state of orgasm all day long. No wonder it's difficult for some priests to keep their pants zipped up.

Pope Francis has asked his flock "to not just believe in Christ but to live out God's 'supernatural' gift of faith in church and society." Now, if God is, as I believe, a manifestation of orgasm, then do we not have a clue as to the nature and origin of faith? How we came to believe blindly (i.e., have faith) in something which isn't there? Orgasm isn't there, it's not something we can see or touch, hear or smell, but what a supernatural gift it is!

He also says that faith illuminates the mind of God. But if faith is orgasmic in nature, is not the mind of God also? And if it's orgasm which illuminates the mind of God, is not man's mind also illuminated by the same source orifice—the sanctification of orgasm (i.e., the mystical transmutation of God)? Is this the devise which got men to think and be wise and eventually be us—Homo sapiens.

Is the mystical union between Christ and His church also the mystical union between orgasm (God) and the pelvis (His church)?

Does the unimpeachable fact that women can experience multiple orgasms (MOs) vs. a man's paltry one have any bearing on women's subjugation from time immemoriable? Did the Phallus become the Word of God inorder to control the MOs of insatiable female ancestors? Is it women that men fear or, in recalling a universal memory (the collective unconscious), the multiple orgasms of women?

And if you peel away the onion, does such a memory lie behind the strong resistance toward such struggles as women's suffrage and the ERA? And why, in some religions, women must sit on one side of the church and men on the other?

Did God morph from a woman's genitalia as well as from the Word of God—i.e., a man's?

God Almighty: Is there anything more almighty than orgasm?

A cathedral is like a magical birth canal. Consider how the nave and transepts and aisles are dwarfed by marble columns and arches carved with flesh-like sinews which tower over us and lead us into the mystery and moment and magic of the Virgin Birth and orgasm sanctified by the Holy Spirit Himself.

If the Church is the womb, perhaps we are all the Virgin Mary and baby Jesus (depending on our gender) when we enter to worship.

Since so many—if not all—origin stories of mankind are sexually charged, is that not a clue that God originated in the pelvis?

(&

If human sacrifices were made in many parts of the ancient world to the tree god (in Germany it was punishable by death to mutilate a tree), what sacrifices might have been made to the God of the Pelvis? When people today want to kill other people whose god is different from theirs, is it the same kind of sacrifice? If we no longer believe that trees are inhabited by spirits, do we still believe that God is the spirit of orgasm?

(&

To say that God is Love, and His love is the strongest force, and His love can squash hate—cannot this also be said of orgasm?

(&

The ongoing debate concerning the origins of human language—how and why it started—need go no further. A powerful clue has just arisen before our very eyes, though it's been out in broad daylight for a couple of thousand years. But, ho hum, sometimes things are so obvious that we walk right past them without ever seeing them. Here is the clue.

"In the beginning was the Word and the Word was with God."

But listen. Long before *this* Word got into the Bible, there was another Word, and *this* Word was with the Phallus of Osiris. What could be more clear? Men and orgasm needed words to control themselves and express themselves. This is *how* language started (i.e., from copulation) and *why* (to control and express copulation). Perhaps we might better say that "In the beginning was the Word and the Word was orgasmic?"

(&

If man was created in the image of God and God was created in the image of orgasm, then what are the ramifications for Civilization itself, founded as it were on the precepts of religious doctrine?

If God resides in the pelvis, if He is the transmutation of orgasm, then He is no delusion; this is why science and religion can co-exist in the same individual's brain.

(&

Does the human perception of reality have its origin in the necessity of transmuting orgasm into God?

(&

Regarding natural selection, what better way to be good at survival and reproduction than to have the best orgasm?

(&

If the brain works in tandem with the reproductive system (i.e., if it is needed for animals to cope with their dangerous environments), then why the human brain developed as it did—language, culture, etc.—can be explained, perhaps, as the result of a reproductive system gone haywire; looked at this way, we should no longer be a mystery.

(&

Does our belief that whatever is beautiful is also good have its roots in the beauty and goodness of orgasm?

And if our belief in physical beauty emanates from a belief in an interior, spiritual beauty, might that belief be coming from the interior of the pelvis?

(&

The Jewish philosopher Maimonides saw God as a presence beyond description. Is that not a perfect metaphor for orgasm—a presence beyond description?

He envisioned a God who reveals himself through nature. Does this sanctification of nature have its origins in the os sacrum, the sanctification of the pelvis? Does the morphing of orgasm reveal itself as God? I.e., does God reveal himself through orgasm?

And because God is perfect, he "reveals himself not through violations of nature (i.e., miracles), but through nature itself." Pray tell, how can orgasm's perfection ever be violated?

Maimonides said that God can't be known through language. Who, pray tell, can describe orgasm?

Intelligence, he said, is a divine gift from God. If man's brain developed in tandem with the sanctification of orgasm, then our intelligence is, indeed, a divine gift from God.

(○)

God's perfection is eternal, orgasm's perfection is fleeting. Could God be our wish for eternal orgasm?

(○)

"There is surely a piece of Divinity in us."
"We carry within us the wonders we seek without us".
      Sir Thomas Browne, author of *Religio Medici* (1642)

(○)

"Beauty is truth, truth beauty"—that is all
Ye know on earth, and all ye need to know.
             John Keats
Can it be that the beauty of orgasm is the only truth we know, and the only truth we need to know?

(○)

Since people who fall into poverty and go to jail are more likely to be perceived as black, and since religion divides the world into good and evil, black and white, is this not an inkling that law and order are rooted in the transference of orgasm into religion—i.e., God?

(○)

If thought has transformed orgasm into God, and the speculation is proven true that thought and consciousness can be explained by the same quantum procedures which compute the navigation of birds, photosynthesis and Nature in general ("the key step in the process involves electrons 'hopping from one molecule to another'"*), then can God Himself be quantumly computed too?

---

* *Life on the Edge* by Johnjoe McFadden & Jim Al-Khalili

When Euripides wrote about the dangerous relationship between man and god, was it to do with the precarious, unresolved issues we have regarding our sexuality? How the god/orgasm syndrome can send us at any moment over the precipice? Make us God-fearing?

☙

If we can agree that all religious terms are rooted in the transmutation of orgasm, then it is much easier to see that a divine messenger is shooting from the pelvis, not the hips. In the Bahai religion, Servenslance, the prophet who called himself the Bab (an Arabic word meaning "the gate") was sublimating the entrance to the pelvis, and his successor, the Baha'ullah ("the glory of God") was totally immersed in the beauty of orgasm.

Are we not all made in a burst of orgasm or, as the Indian swami Paramahansa Yogananda has said, in the image of God?

☙

A pastor tells his Spanish-speaking congregation that "God is here in L.A. as you struggle. God is there with your family in Mexico and Guatemala..." By the magical transference of orgasm into God, what he says is true.

He also says, "If you trust in Jesus, you are completely perfect." Because orgasm is perfect, by its magical transference into Jesus, what the pastor says is true.

Might it be that the species which have the best orgasms are the ones which have the best reproductive success?

(〇

The Redeemer will bring perfect freedom. Does not orgasm do the same?

(〇

God is in every man. Is not orgasm in every man also?

(〇

Does the threat of "godless communism" play less to a man's intellect than to his pelvis? Is the fear of communism the fear of what might happen to Civilization once the magical transference of God and orgasm is broken?

(〇

In some religious traditions and cultures, the winter solstice brings "havoc and evil" on the longest day of the year. Now if Evil has its source in the duality of religion, and orgasm is the source of religion, do our celebrations at the end of the year—honoring the dead on Halloween, sacrificing animals on Thanksgiving, and celebrating the birth of a doomed god on Christmas—all owe their existence to orgasm and a primeval fear of it?

(〇

If heaven is the transmogrification of orgasmic ecstasy, and orgasm can be perceived as a sort of out-of-body-dying experience, no wonder there are those who believe that martyrdom is a direct route to heaven!

(〇

That the concept of Divine Will has been used to govern the people of Russia throughout its history is not hard to understand. The Kremlin itself, fortified by the candy cane turrets and sugar plum domes of St. Basil's Cathedral, bespeaks of the delicious sweetness of orgasm and all its preternatural / magical power.

Is that universal feeling known as sexual guilt rooted in the Oedipal complex, or (if God is the transfiguration of orgasm) in our embarrassment as we slither and slide under His watchful eye?

Transfiguration: A radical change in form or appearance. A change that glorifies or exalts. A metamorphosis.

Metamorphosis: A transformation, as by magic or sorcery.

But no matter. What better way to glorify and exalt orgasm than through God? And how better to glorify and exalt God than through orgasm?

❧

How beautiful is thy dwelling place, O Lord!
Psalm 84:1
Perhaps no truer words were ever spoken.

❧

At the height of Mayan civilization, when a king met defeat in battle, why were the hands of his scribes—those instruments which created the words, paintings and sculptures which glorified the king's divinity—mutilated in public, their fingers broken and fingernails torn out, if words and art—i.e., culture—were not born of the same clothas God—i.e., the transmogrification of orgasm?

❧

"If nothing dies there is no resurrection." That is, you can't have an erect penis without first having a flaccid one...

❧

21

When a baby boy is having a spontaneous erection, is it due to a sudden surge of testosterone or the glorious presence of God?

During the reign of Pope John Paul II, who frequently referred to Satan as a dangerous force in the world, the Vatican's top exorcist used the following tools to perform exorcisms: a crucifix (the symbol of Oedipal desire?), an aspergillum (symbolizing the phallus?) and a container of baptismal oil (symbolic of semen?). Is it possible that this dangerous force is located in the pelvis?

In the 7th century, Christian refugees fleeing persecution in Jerusalem came to Cappadocia in central Turkey and settled in an area of towering phallic-like tufts which the locals today call the "Love Valley." Does the connection between God and orgasm get any better than this?

If God is indeed a mystical emanation of orgasm, then no wonder an overwhelming majority of Americans continue to believe that heaven exists; what could be better than a state of eternal existence in God's presence, as 46% of people believe heaven to be?

And what better way to sublimate orgasm than that of the Second Coming, the notion that believers in Jesus will be carried up to God in what is known as the Rapture—i.e., the state of being transported by a lofty emotion such as ecstasy from on place to another, especially to heaven.

For many Christians, the Book of Revelations serves as God's countdown to his son's return to Earth for a final triumph over evil. But what is the evil? What is the triumph? That the son will finally be able to overcome his Oedipal desire for his mother? Or, perhaps, that the desire will no longer be seen as evil....?

(Q

Where does racism come from? Is it when men struggling to overcome the dark side of their sexuality—the side that wants to rape and pillage and consummate forbidden unions—enslave the darker races instead?

(Q

When an Amish church-goer, admittedly suffering from sexual guilt and hatred of God, enters a school-house and shoots 11 girls; when a man undresses before a church altar and proclaims himself to be Jesus Christ; when a Catholic priest strangles a nun and makes an upside-down cross on her body with a letter-opener; and when a woman, thinking the Catholic church has it in for her, enters and kills the priest—can we infer that, at least for these four people, the mystical connection between God and orgasm has become pathological? Is the transmutation of orgasm into God in itself pathological?

Birth canal at St. Peters

According to the Apostolic United Brethren and other fundamentalist offshoots of the Mormon church, the practice of polygamy "brings exaltation in heaven" and confers "heaven's highest blessing." Now if God is, indeed, the mystical transmutation

of orgasm, then does it not seem a no-brainer that the more wives one has, the more orgasm one has—i.e., exaltation in heaven?

(&

If God's kingdom exists within the pelvis, and the purpose of the Messiah is to restore God's kingdom, then Jesus as the Messiah is here to restore—what? Something to do with our forbidden sexual desires? And since he is the Deliverer and Savior, is he here to deliver us to them or save us from them? Or could it be something else...

(&

"Following the expulsion of the Jews from Spain in 1492, there was a policy of eliminating every symbol or memory of their presence in the country."*

I.e., get rid of the old patriarchal God. Let us only see his Son who was crucified, and who reminds us of our incestuous thoughts and forbidden desires. The pain is so sweet, so rewarding.

(&

If God is orgasm, can anything be more mystical (or absurd!) than seeking Him through self-denial?

(&

When people talk about the greatness of God, are they really giving obeisance to the greatness of orgasm?

(&

In Catholicism, orgasm must be experienced naturally—i.e., without contraceptives. To do otherwise is to tamper with God. Those who sanction the use of contraceptives "will invoke divine wrath on themselves." Does that mean orgasm that is angry at being tampered with?

* Archeology Magazine", September/October 2013

Before molesting him, a Catholic priest puts his hands on a young man's genitals and says, "This is like mine because I am your father and I am taking care of you."

What he means is "I am God and orgasm is my business."

In the beginning was the Word and the Word was with God and the Word was God.

I can't help but wonder whether or not the Word and the penis are the same thing. Was not God, in the old days, the embodiment of the Divine Phallus? Whose "straightness," significant as "a rule of measure," led to the concept of universal order and balance, truth and justice? Was not the loss of the Word symbolized by the phallus of the Egyptian god Osiris?

And the Word became flesh and dwelt among us, full of grace and truth....

Is the flesh the penis? Is grace the beauty of orgasm? Is truth the measure of it all? When we spread the Word of God, are we really talking (subconsciously, of course) about orgasm? Or, perhaps, the lost phallus of Osiris?

When the first Christians (still acutely aware of their pagan contemporaries) gathered each Sunday—the Lord's Day, the Resurrection Day—to celebrate Jesus' resurrection, were they thinking, essentially, about erections, too? Is this what Easter and Good Friday are all about?

If the bedrock of Christianity rests upon the musty theme of Oedipal desire between mother and son, as exemplified by the Crucifixion;* and if the bedrock of Judaism rests upon the rite of

---

* Georg Groddeck, *The Book of the It*

circumcision—i.e., the Covenant between God and Abraham, can we not say that the God of orgasm is behind it all?

It is hard to imagine how our ape-like ancestors, those still living in trees but already endowed with a human pelvis (as was Australopithecus sediba)—how they were able to cope with orgasm. Perhaps they couldn't. Perhaps the chaos which ensued is described in the Bible as "the darkness upon the face of the deep." And perhaps this helps explain how orgasm became the Spirit of God who said "Let there be light," thus ending the chaos and an earth adrift "without form and void."

If God is orgasm—i.e., if the mystical experience of orgasm has been transmogrified, transformed into the mystical experience of God, then might it not follow that every word in the Bible gets its power from the mystical experience of orgasm?

In other words, is the bedrock of all Biblical teaching—hence our sense of right and wrong and our belief in morality, orgasmic in origin? Are the following admonitions (chosen at random) a result of this unique transportation? Perhaps the fear of orgasm, transmuted into the fear of God, is what made people obey...

Exodus 23:9
"You must not oppress the stranger, you know how a stranger feels, for you lived as strangers in the land of Egypt."

Timothy 2:14
"Have nothing to do with stupid, senseless controversies; you know that they breed quarrels"

If the experience of orgasm by our prehistoric ancestors caused many alarming problems, wouldn't the fear of it need to be mystically transmuted, too, not just the glory? And would this fear become what we call Evil?

"How lovely is Thy dwelling place, O Lord!"
Does the connection between God and orgasm get any better than this?

Or this, as when Plotinus talks about the Divine Form from which all things emanate including beauty: "This is the spirit that beauty must ever induce: wonderment and a delicious trouble, longing and love and a trembling that is all delight."

(&

"I've always felt God was inside me."

(&

If heaven is, as many believe, "a state of eternal existence in God's presence," are we possibly dreaming about an eternity of orgasm?

St. Teresa by Giovanni Bernini

If religion has not grown out of our own bodies, then why were the Torahs—the holy books of Judaism which roll up into phallic-like scrolls— buried once they became damaged and unholy—i.e., like a body that would putrefy?

(&

And if religion is, really, a physical manifestation, if it is a consequence of atoms and molecules, cells and raging hormones, then to believe otherwise, to believe that religion is something intangible, spiritual, unearthly, is this not a form of deception? And are any deceptions ever good for our well-being?

(&

When the doors of heaven open.....
Could the exquisite moment of orgasm be described more poetically than this?

(&

If in the old days there were spirits living in everything—trees, rocks, brooks, mountains—why not in the pelvis?

Birth canal at Basilica of St. Therese

Is it possible that people will go to war on the pretext of religious differences when, in fact, everybody's God is the same, namely orgasm?

(&

God is goodness. (Is there anything "more good" than orgasm?)

If God and goodness reside in the pelvis, then it seems logical that His opposite—Lucifer, the devil, evil, badness—resides there, too. Is the key to all the horrors and atrocities people commit, to be found in the pelvis?

And does a disconnect from the goodness of orgasm—i.e., from God and the way we are supposed to treat each other—open a person up to crime—i.e., to acts of bad orgasm such as rape and murder? Is the source of all havoc, no matter what the rationale—ideological, political, etc.—rooted in the pelvis?

℘

Does the *os sacrum* hold the key to matters affecting the soul?

Is the mystery of God also the mystery of orgasm?

℘

When we see images of a fetus pleasuring itself in the womb, is there any doubt that God is in all of us, possibly from the moment of conception?

℘

If the belief in God is rooted in man's mystical experience of orgasm, then perhaps that's why Pope Benedict XVI, feeling demoralized over revelations of a gay lobby in the Vatican, decided to forge a deeper relationship with God and get out of the papacy, quick.

℘

And then there is Pope Francis who kept secret for several years, and for reasons, he has said, that are unclear even to him, the decision he made when he was seventeen to become a priest after God spoke to him in church one day. Now if God is, possibly, that mystical eminence emanating from orgasm, would not this and a guilty conscience emanating from raging hormones explain everything?

℘

If the worldly splendor and exquisite trappings of the Catholic church help to form part of our "experience of the divine," and to affirm the pope's role as God's representative on Earth, are they not, essentially, a tool used to sanctify orgasm? And by substituting golden hats and mitres and chalices encrusted with precious stones to express the ineffable beauty of orgasm, is this not the "the glorious role of the church?"

And is this why a feeling of peace comes over us inside a church? Does not orgasm, as it lifts us out of our earthly bodies, give us a respite from all the cares that existence brings with it, and a foretaste of eternal peace?

Is orgasm the bedrock of this terrible/wonderful thing we call Civilization? I.e., was the need to control orgasm the catalyst which led to the evolution of a species which devised Civilization?

(☙

When the Creator bathes in a Sacred Lake, as He often does in various world mythologies, people believe that the lake has a healing force. Now, if the Creator happens merely to be an embodiment of the Phallus, wouldn't the Sacred Lake be the lubricating waters of the Vagina?

Or, put in another way, if it's actually the Phallus who is passing Himself off as the Creator, is it not likely that the Vagina is therefore passing Herself off as the Sacred Lake?

(☙

If the Word of God is religious-speak for the Phallus; and if the etymological origins for the word King is also phallic-derived (Latin *rex*, a king, from *rectus*, straight, and *regere*, to guide in a straight

line—(a penis?)—then the concept of kingship as divinely ordained is not far from the truth afterall.

Why did the ancient Mayans embed sharp objects such as stingray spines into the genitalia of their kings and queens—i.e., those who were the earthly representatives of God—if religion wasn't connected to the power of orgasm? Or, more precisely, if God's abode wasn't in the pelvis?

(◊)

In the Gnostic Gospel of Judas, Jesus confides to Judas: "Step away from the others and I shall tell you the mysteries of the kingdom. It is possible for you to reach it, but you will grieve a great deal."

The mysteries of the kingdom. What are they? The mysteries of orgasm in the kingdom of the father? If God is rooted in the pelvis—*the os sacrum,* the sacred bone — is Jesus letting Judas into the secret of Oedipal desires? And since these desires are forbidden, is the Son of God setting Judas up to betray him as a warning against these desires?

Again, in the Gnostic Gospel of Judas, Judas exceeds all the other disciples because he will help Jesus get rid of his flesh and liberate the divine being within. Now if this divine being within us is Oedipal in nature, is this why Judas will "be cursed by other generations"?

(◊)

Is the Catholic ritual of dipping a finger in the blessed waters and making the sign of the Cross symbolic of the watery effluence during sexual intercourse and our forbidden desires which may be represented by the Crucifix?[*]

(◊)

When our ancestors came down from the trees and began to walk, their spines newly aligned and their pelvises broadened, was the stage set for a new kind of orgasm? And if so, did a sea change take place in the natural world?

[*] op. cit. *Book of the It*

Researchers have shown what can happen to a mouse if he's allowed to pleasure himself to death. Now since we have the same chromosomes and genes as a mouse (and apparently cockroaches, too), couldn't our ancestors have become equally obsessed? Did the human mind and civilization evolve from the chaotic mess of unbridled orgasm?

While it may seem inconceivable, even preposterous that something as carnal as orgasm could have morphed into such a transcendent being as God, yet how strange it is that so many of the descriptions we use to try and define God can just as easily be used to adequately (or inadequately!) define orgasm.

Luke 17:21

"The kingdom of God is within you." Indeed, perhaps it is!

Matthew 3:2

*"Repent ye: for the kingdom of heaven is at hand."** And closer than we think?*

Did that blackened fertile delta known as pubic hair give rise to the symbolism of a burning bush—an inextinguishable fire (read sexual desire) from which God spoke and gave Moses the Ten Commandments (i.e., our laws regarding sexual desire and behavior?).

---

* Some translations substitute the word heaven for God. Either way, how better to transubstantiate the physical yet indefinable beauty of orgasm into something intangible?

And by making God's name so sacrosanct (any book containing it must never be destroyed or effaced), is this not a way of keeping people in holy terror of God, hence a grand way of keeping man's libido under lock and key if, indeed, he has confused God with orgasm?

Is this terror of God the secret of religion? Is the secret of religion the terror of orgasm?

In orthodox Judaism, the ancient name for God is never pronounced out loud. Is it a mere coincidence that, until recently, the same dictum applied to the words penis, vagina and orgasm?

Is it God we are praising in church and Sunday school, or the divine knowledge of orgasm?

If racism is not rooted in religion, in the concept of the duality of religion—Good and Evil, the Darkness versus the Light—then why did Mormon doctrine hold, until recently, that blacks were not deemed "temple worthy," an edict which prohibited them from applying to sing with the famous Tabernacle Choir?

But if God and orgasm are interchangeable, the Mormon doctrine of polygamy is indeed an ingenuous way of "shedding forth the precious light of heaven," as the Mormon leaders said to the Choir back in 1895.

Has the Supreme Moment become the Supreme Being? That is for us all to ponder.

There will never be peace amongst men as long as God's Word is synonymous with the phallus.

(⟳

If the Rule of Law has its origins in religion, and if religion was established to curtail the overwhelming power of orgasm, then it comes to this, that our lives are not determined by free will but by biological forces beyond our control.

(⟳

It is as difficult to grasp the existence of a supreme being as it is to grasp the existence of orgasm

(⟳

"God gives you strength." So does orgasm.

(⟳

Wallace Stevens said that God and the imagination are one. Could our experience of orgasm be the way to imagining Him?

(⟳

When we enter a church, whether we are believers or not, we become believers temporarily because we know orgasm to be true.

God can't be described, and neither can orgasm.

(⟳

Were the seeds of anti-Semitism sown when the ancient Hebrews stopped worshipping orgasm in the guise of the Golden Calf, and conceptualized it instead as an abstact entity, thus ending the world's practice of paganism?

Note that the name Israel means "one who struggled with God and overcame." Overcame what, man's struggle with orgasm?

&

If Civilization is dependent on the foundation of religion, and if religion is, simply put, rooted within the confines of the pelvis, then does this not bespeak of the overarching reach of orgasm in all walks of life? All the edifices, all the artifice?

&

If orgasm is indeed that diety who oscilates inside the pelvis, then no wonder the people of the ancient world believed they could be in direct communication with their gods. Or that Martin Luther surmised a thousand years later that God's grace came not through the church but direct to each believer.

&

Are the elaborate retablos which rise above the altar of a church, sometimes as high as forty feet or more, our attempt to capture the sublime glory of orgasm and thus channel libidinous desires through God?

Altar at Notre Dame Cathedral

Now that we are in the space age, a theological debate with many farreaching questions as to whether or not alien souls need saving, has many Christians biting their nails. But if the reproductive organs of extraterrestrials aren't the same as ours, might such proselytizing only be a waste of time?

"We are gathered here in the sight of God." Would this preamble to our wedding ceremonies be so powerful if not rooted in the power of orgasm? Ditto, when we say that the eye of God is upon us?

(&

Could orgasm lead us to a new understanding of the Divine? And could a new understanding of the Divine—i.e., the Ultimate Climax—bring about a better understanding of ourselves and a more peaceful world to boot?

(&

Is it merely a coincidence that cathedrals often rely on such heavily veined stones as alabaster which, with little stretch of the imagination, resemble the veins of living tissue? Are we thus transported magically into the mystery of the womb?

(&

The word "rapture" comes from rapere, "to carry off, abduct, seize, take forcefully." At the end of time, when the Christian Rapture takes place, is it God who will forcefully carry the believers up to heaven, or orgasm?

(&

The Judeo-Christian tradition teaches us that good and evil are symbolized by light and darkness. Thus "to walk in the light of the Lord"—i.e., to grow in holiness—involves the removal of darkness or that which gratifies sin. With this message so deeply imbedded in childhood, can one really blame the police, our keepers of law and order—i.e., public morality, social control—for shooting down the dark-skinned races, especially the young virile blacks?

In a policeman's subconscious mind (and the minds of all who adhere to the duality of religion), is that not the Biblically-correct thing to do?

(&

The Inexpressible is both orgasm and God. God is the ultimate climax.

⟨⟨⟩

In the moment of orgasm we are freed of all conflict. Is that not what we expect from our relationship with God?

⟨⟨⟩

Why do people protect their gods? Unknowingly, they are the pleasure of orgasm, and who wants to loose orgasm?

⟨⟨⟩

Is orgasm the true word of God?

⟨⟨⟩

If art is an expression of the ineffable, then surely it is rooted in orgasm.

⟨⟨⟩

The mystery of God is the mystery of orgasm.

⟨⟨⟩

If religion isn't rooted in orgasm, then why have artists depicted so many biblical figures without their clothes on?

⟨⟨⟩

If the awareness of self depends on the mental sensation of the electric and chemical flows in our bodies, might not our ancestors have been dumbfounded on becoming bi-pedal and experiencing a radically different orgasm? (I.e., a straight shot up the spine?)

And since we appear to be the only species with culture, and the only species featuring a pelvis that is in a direct line to the brain which results, perhaps, in an electrifying—language, art, politics, etc.—be the indirect result of our anatomical makeup?

⟨⟨⟩

In the Kaballah, demons are born when men misuse their generative power. Does this mean that evil arises from orgasm gone awry?

(♑

When Moses asks God what his name is, God says: "I am who I am." In defining orgasm, one could say: "It is what it is."

(♑

The Holy Ark is the cabinet in which the scrolls of the Torah, the divine knowledge of the Jewish religion, are kept protected. The word *ark* comes from *arcere*: to contain or maintain at a distance, to keep or ward off, possibly "I prevent." One wonders what is being magically warded off. What were the ancient Hebrews trying to prevent? If, by chance, the cabinet (the enclosed box) represents the female, and the rolled up scrolls represent the male, was this a way to sanctify orgasm?

(♑

The God of Heaven in ancient Syria was called El. The word Israel comes from "el," God, and "yisra," to fight, to struggle. In the Bible, a man named Jacob struggles with an angel and is subsequently renamed "Israel," "he who struggles with God." Now if the hypothesis is correct, if orgasm is the source of God—i.e., of all that is holy to mankind—then Jacob was struggling with man's sexual appetites. Appetites going back millions of years and unabated to this day. (For a vivid description of Australopithecus' murderous high jinks, see Raymond Dart's "Adventures With the Missing Link," pgs. 106-119.)

> "You have striven with God and with men,
> and have prevailed." Genesis, chpt. 32

Is it possible that herein lies the cause of anti-Semitism, that ugliest of human passions? If the human subconscious would prefer to worship orgasm not with a stern and invisible God, but, as in antiquity, with many gods, some licentious and jolly, others blood-thirsty with an appetite for human sacrifice, could the need to eradicate Jewish culture be linked to the introduction of the one God—i.e., via Jacob's struggle with orgasm and his success in reigning it in, not only for himself but

for all mankind? That the hatred of anti-Semitism is so palpable, so visceral, so irrational—the thought that it eminates from the gonads may not be far-fetched at all.

⟨&⟩

When we obliterate what is perceived as an inherent evil, I have heard it expressed as light triumphing over darkness, or "light overwhelming darkness." *Overwhelming*. The physical aspect of this powerful word can't be ignored, nor the likelihood that the black races represent all our fears, which is why they are targeted so freely.

⟨&⟩

How can we not connect orgasm with God—or better yet, orgasm with magic and then with God, for surely it was through magic that the transition was achieved—when there are so many clues? If the essence of magic consists of the direct control by man of the forces of nature,* what better method to control orgasm, a most awesome force of nature, than by magic? Indeed, perhaps orgasm laid the very foundation for magic.

And since magic invests its practitioners with social power and acts as a source of social control, could the ultimate source of society be rooted in the channeling of orgasm?

⟨&⟩

No one seems to know why or how language evolved, but if the backbone of magic is the spell and the ritual, perhaps herein lies the answer to its evolution, a need for words in order to control orgasm. "In the beginning was the Word, and the Word was with God, and the Word was God." Is it mere coincidence that both the Old and New Testament mention the Word of God nearly five hundred times, or is it the way magic spells are supposed to work? A spell which, in Ezekiel alone, is repeated 63 times: "The word of the Lord came again unto me, saying..."

⟨&⟩

*Main source for passages on magic: the Encyclopedia Britannica, Volume 11, 1943.

Within the Word, has the magician, the sorceror, controlled the force of orgasm? In Egypt, the Word was symbolized by the phallus of Osiris, god of fertility: "Homage to thee...Osiris whose word is truth..."

(◌

Are the Christian hymns and prayers, which are sung and spoken at sunrise and sunset, modeled after the Egyptian hymns and prayers to Ra, which were also spoken at sunrise and sunset?

(◌

Simon Magus wanted to be baptized because he thought it was a ritual which held a magic power superior to his own.

(◌

Noam Chomsky believed that languages are a by-product of the innate biology of our brain. Since the brain controls the gonads (unless it is the other way around), and if religion (i.e., the sanctifying of orgasm) is the source of culture, then can language be seen as a by-product of the gonads? Perhaps the etymology of the following words* will help shine a light on language as a source of magical control. Let us see...

Heresy: to seize, to take, especially for oneself. (Original object a woman?)

Dominus the Lord: from domus (house) and dominus (the master of the house).

Pudendum (the external genital organs of either sex): from pudere, to be ashamed, to feel ashamed.

Vulva: refers to curved, enclosing objects. A well. The Well of the Virgin?

Woman: the vibrator. He trembles, he vibrates.

Vagina: a sheath. (Hence a man's love of swords?)

Penis: the withinner, the penetrator.

---

* Source: Origins by Eric Partridge, Macmillan Co. 1958: American Heritage Dictionary, Houghton Mifflin Co. 1976; Word Origins and their Romantic Stories. by Wilfred Funk, Grosset & Dunlap, 1950.

Testicle: from testament, a witness to virility. (Hence the source for the Old and New Testament?)

Resurrection: to surge, to move in a swelling manner. Could there be a connection between the surging (resurrection) of a flaccid penis, and Christ's rising (resurrection) from the dead?

Religion: to bind with ligaments. (Maybe human ligaments?)

Rex (a king); to guide or direct in a straight line (in imitation of the phallus?). Does the king's power come from the sanctifying of orgasm?

Sadhu (a holy man): from straight, right, holy. I.e., that which is straight is right, and that which is right is straight. (Kind of like saying a good man is hard to find and a hard man is good to find?)

Right: from rex. Straight, stretched upright, hence that which is fitting and good.

Sinister: on the left, hence unfavorable to the right. In Old Norse, sannr (sin) meant true but also guilty.

True: from tree, straight as a tree. (Or an erect penis?)

&

Could the sacred metre—i.e., the regularity of the rhythm and cadence of words—mentioned in certain scriptures, be patterned on the rhythmic movement of the male within the female?

&

Is our magnificent Civilization nothing more than hocus pocus?

&

If religion isn't rooted in orgasm, than why is there an obelisk (i.e., a phallic symbol) in the middle of St. Peter's Square?

&

Did all our dietary religious laws come about as a deterrent to our ancestors' practice of eating each other?

&

After pulling himself out of the waters of the Abyss (vagina, perhaps?), the supreme god of Egypt created more gods by masturbating.

(◌

Evolutionary psychologists hold that the brain did not evolve for reading and writing. But did reading and writing evolve to make orgasm holy?

(◌

If a king's power to rule has been transmogrified from the power of orgasm, is it also the source of power inherent in all governing bodies?

(◌

God is the cosmic force which sets the laws of nature in motion, and orgasm is the biological force which sets the laws of nature in motion.

(◌

The word "money" is derived from the name of the Roman goddess Moneta (a.k.a. the goddess Juno) in whose temple the Romans made their coins.* The state and the deity were synonymous, giving sacred qualities to the currency of all ancient civilizations. Assuming that the idea of sanctity originates in the gonads, is our obsession with money and wealth orgasmic in nature?

(◌

I place my theory for the transmogrification of orgasm into God (through the articulation of magic words and rituals) not from the time of the earliest known civilizations and written languages, such as Sumerian (3300-3000 BC); not from the recent claim of 70,000-100,000 years ago for the origin of language; but from the recent evidence that, some 25 million years ago, an ancestor common to both humans and baboons had the ability to articulate vowel-like sounds, a necessity for the development of human speech. In 25 million years, anything can happen!

* (New Yorker Magazine, "Annals of Finance," November 9, 1987.

Of course there could be no orgasmic connection between the putto, the naked male child who, in classical times, represented erotic love—hence, Cupid—and the putto who came to represent in later times the sacred cherub and the omnipresence of God. Even the fact that they're both winged is surely just coincidence.

(&

"What is the Book of Life itself but man's war with nature?"* Could that war, perhaps, be with the power of orgasm?

(&

Is mimesis, the imitation or representation of nature, especially in art and literature, our way of channeling orgasm, or our way of opposing Civilization and all its constraints?

(&

God as Prime Mover: is there a mover more prime than ogasm?

(&

In the ancient Persian religion, it was Arta the god of Truth who gave form and beauty to the Universe. Now, if the earliest incarnation of Truth was the Phallus—later the Light of Truth or the Word of God—then did these concepts of form and beauty evolve from the external force of orgasm?

(&

The ritual of baptism goes back at least to ancient Egypt where it was thought that holy water (i.e., water sancitied by the priests) carried divine life and was the necessary conduit for meeting God. Could the vascular duct be the conduit to God and the basis for baptism?

(&

* 1942 film "The Jungle Book"

What makes the clergy so very different from us? They are immersed in orgasm 24/7, whereas we are immersed in it only on occasion.

Many laws governing orgasm are to be found in Leviticus.

Organized religion is organized orgasm.

Matrimony is another way of governing orgasm: two people patrolling each other's forever until death do them part.

Animals have no gods. When we were animals, we had no gods. Now that we do, where did they come from, and why?

Now I ask you. What is that obelisk, that symbol of an erect penis, doing infront of St. Peter's Basilica?

If only there had been some nuance in the Bible; without its strict doctrine of dualism—of Good and Evil, the moral symbolism of Darkness and Light—surely racism would have had a better chance of being nipped in the bud than it has had otherwise.

Through access to an external mystical force, it is believed that religious rituals can influence both human and natural events. What is more external, what is more mystical, than orgasm? Is this the conduit through which civilization evolved?

The Renaissance philosopher Marsilio Ficino, in adapting Diotoma's ladder of love* to Christian theology, believed that love of the divine could be achieved through love of a single person.

(I.e., through sensual beauty at the lowest rung—i.e., orgasm—we are able to perceive the true and heavenly beauty which dwells in the innermost recesses of God—i.e., Holy Orgasm, orgasm sanctified.)

❧

Does our belief in hell (see Hieronymus Bosch's painting,"The Gates of Hell") come from the Scriptures, or from a universal unconscious memory of human life before there was magic?

❧

In the Mayan creation myth, the Popol Vul, language was created so that the magnificent power of the gods could be praised. This frequent juxtaposition of words and power, words and truth—truth being synonymous with the gods and God—does it not give us a glimmer into deep-time, and a clue that, if orgasm *is* synonymous with God, the power of orgasm was the catalyst behind language?

❧

At the moment of orgasm's release, when we feel that perfect yet fleeting sense of peace and relief—has it been magically transformed into the same feeling of perfect peace and release which comes over us when we enter a House of God? And the longer we stay there, the longer it stays with us?

❧

"I saw in his hand a long spear of gold, and at the point there seemed to be a little fire. He appeared to me to be thrusting it at times into my heart, and to pierce my very entrails. When he drew it out, he seemed to draw them out also, and to leave me all on fire with a great love of God. The pain was so great that it made me moan, and yet so surpassing was the sweetness of this excessive pain, that I could not wish to be rid of it...."

---

* In Plato's Symposium, the philosopher Diotoma explains how, by loving the beautiful things on earth, one steps higher and higher until one reaches the divine knowledge of beauty itself.

St. Teresa of Avila

In Saint Teresa's vision of God, has a more poetic and glorious description of a woman's orgasm ever been written?

If I were to write a hymn to orgasm, could I choose a better vehicle than this Christian hymn, the "Gloria in excelsis Deo" ("Glory to God in the Highest")?

> Glory be to God on High.....
> We praise Thee, we bless Thee,
> We worship Thee, we glorify Thee,
> We give thanks to Thee, for Thy great glory....

Pope Francis has said that the church is a woman. I go a step further and say that the church is a woman's womb.

Were the artists of yore expressing a subconscious allusion to sexual transport—i.e., orgasm—when painting their beatific visions of virgins ascending to heaven?

When an alleged culprit is apprehended by the police, then pounced upon—choked, kicked, etc., even killed—is this the result of an uncontrollable urge to punish the miscreant, or a visceral out-pouring of self-hatred rooted in the need to punish their own unacceptable and unresolvable conflicts, probably of a sexual nature?

If orgasm has given us the impetus for language—hence, speech—might it not also be the impetus for art—i.e., the desire to capture it visually? From cave art and petroglyphs (yes, magical or religious but rooted in orgasm) to today's modern art, so abstract because no longer under the umbrella of the Church, is our desire to capture "the majesty of divine creation" none but the truth of each artist's vision inspired by the unrefutable truth of orgasm?

Just as God may be ensconced in orgasm (how else explain our ancestors' belief that they were descended from the gods?) so may the universal memory of our primate past be lost in it.

The moral symbolism of light has, no doubt, led to the destruction of many lives unfortunately embedded within dark skins.

If we truly believe in God and the Scriptures, in the Word of God and His Son, then, should it turn out that God is but a lovely metaphore, a transformation from something else (so many times discussed in these pages), then it may not be wrong to say that the Bible is a very cunning book.

But then, why not? It was written by men, and are we not a cunning species? Are we not adept at deception and conniving as are so many other species in the Animal Kingdom?

And if cunning weren't going on, then why the age-old fear of science? The fear of ideas that threaten to de-sanctify the divine quality of nature? Was Bruno burned at the stake, rather than have the deception revealed?

⟨◌⟩

What a grand joke it would be on those who make a career of analyzing and interpreting Scripture—from monks to theologians to professors and professors emeritus—if they are pondering nothing more or less than the highest point of sexual excitment—orgasm.

⟨◌⟩

If the sacred and the secular are identical, why cleave them apart? Surely it only makes for trouble!

⟨◌⟩

The Transcendentalists believed in a direct connection to the divine through nature. How better to connect to the divine than through orgasm!

⟨◌⟩

The American Heritage Dictionary defines religion as the expression of man's belief in and reverence for a superhuman power[*] recognized as the creator or governor of the universe. Could we not pare down this definition considerably by simply saying that religion is the inextricable connection between God and orgasm?

---

[*] In another AHD edition: supernatural power or powers

God is perfect. Is there anything more perfect than orgasm?

In Conclusion

In 200 BC, the Imperial Palace of Weiyang was built by Emperor Gaozu of China. In order to evoke its religious intent, Weiyang, also known as the Endless Palace, was built along specific axial and symmetrical lines. This would assure harmony between nature and the people.

The dictionary gives the definition of axis as a straight line about which a body or geometrical object rotates or may be conceived to rotate. Now, since the same definiton of axis could be applied to the penis rotating inside the vagina, was this the real axis the Emperor was giving devotion to? It's climax as endless as the palace itself?

Symmetry is defined as beauty as a result of balance or harmonious arrangement. In that harmonious arrangement, that perfect balance between the male and female symmetry which releases orgasm, can such beauty ever be surpassed?

Reach down to the gonads and you will find the source of all man's beneficence and all his ills. See how the hierarchy of magicians and priests, originally established to control orgasm, has produced an artificial caste system and a world of riches and poverty.

> "The rich man in his castle,
> The poor man at his gate,
> God made them high and lowly
> And ordered their estate."*

See how, in ancient civilizations, the molds and kilns and wombs of goddesses were worshipped as one; the edifices thus built with these sacred mortar stones and bricks were now embued with the sanctity of the womb.

* All Things Bright and Beautiful. Anglican hymn.

Which came first, the asylum we are offered in the sanctuary of Mother Church, or the asylum our own mothers gave us in the sanctuary of her womb?

See how the intertwining tendrils and calligraphic curlicues of the arabesque mimic and celebrate those follicular curlicues we call pubic hair. What is modern art but a new way to express, to imitate the power and beauty and glory of orgasm, now freed from the restraints from its religious beginnings?

Listen to the words of the first songs ever written—they celebrate the liberating effect of wine on man's libido.

Would language be so powerful, so lethal, capable of insighting us to horrendous deeds and crimes, if it weren't born of our fear of God—i.e., the power of orgasm? The ideologies that call for total destruction of a system (a futile attempt to upend our taboos) will then call for total order because the taboos can only be tweeked but never upended.

In conclusion I offer a word I've not used before. The dictionary defines numen as 1. The presiding divinity or spirit (of a place). 2. The spirit believed by animists to inhabit certain natural objects. 3. Creative energy regarded as a genius or demon dwelling within one.

The place, the natural obect, I suggest to be the gonads and the pelvis—the "os sacrum." The creative energy is orgasm. When we are told that God is the force by which we become our highest, truest self, orgasm (disguised as the numen) fits the bill. To transcend to a higher, spiritual plane, orgasm—the numen—fits the bill. When religious faith is defined as the belief in something we cannot see, the numen—orgasm—fits the bill.

From pelvis to brain, from orgasm to God; from hominids eating each other to Jesus Christ offering his body in a wafer; from knuckle-dragging monkeys to bi-pedal apes—i.e., people—it's been a long journey along a very dark road. If I've helped clear things up a bit, the effort was worth it.

C.F. Hayes

Bibliography

Dear Reader: The books listed below, and others perhaps not listed, have helped me in determining the direction of my thoughts. Without them I could not have formulated the heretofore unexpressed idea that orgasm—that impossible-to-describe, identify or explain sensory experience—is what channeled our ancestors—perhaps so primitive they were hardly out of the trees—toward a belief in a supernatural world in which a supernatural being reigned whom today we identify as God. That there is substance to the speculation may hopefully be perceived from the list below.

The Sacred Books of the East, edited by F. Max Muller: The Zend-Avesta, Parts I-III; The Palavi Texts, Parts I-V: Motilal Banarsidass Press, India.

An Introduction to Ancient Iranian Religion, trans. by William W. Malandra: University of Minnesota Press, Minneapolis 1983.

Phrase and Word Origins, by Alfred H. Holt: Dover Press, NY 1961.

Numbers, Their Meaning and Magic, by Isodore Kozminsky: Samuel Weiser Inc., NY 1980.

On the Kabbalah and Its Symbolism, by Gershom Scholem: Schocken Books, NY 1978.

The Perfumed Garden of Shaykh Nefzawi, trans. by Sir Richard Burton: G.P. Putnam's Sons, NY 1963

Adventures with the Missing Link, by Raymond A. Dart: Harper & Brothers, NY 1959.

Egypt Handbook, by Kathy Hanson: Moon Publications Inc., Chico, Ca. 1993.

The Book of the It, by Georg Groddeck: The New American Library, NY 1961.

The Lost Keys of Freemasonry, by Manly P. Hall: Macoy Publishing & Masonic Supply Co. Inc, Richmond, Vir. 1976.

The Mysteries of Mithra, by Franz Cumont: Dover Publications Inc., NY 1956.

The Origin of Consciousness in the Breakdown of the Bicameral Mind, by Julian James: Houghton Mifflin Co. Boston 1990.

The Road To Man, by Herbert Wendt: Doubleday & Co., NY 1959.

Origins Reconsidered, by Richard Leakey: Doubleday, NY 1992.

Introduction to Physiological Psychology, by Francis Leukel Ph.D., The C.V. Mosby Co., Saint Louis 1972.

Images of Lust, by Anthony Weir and James Jerman: Routledge, London and New York, 1986.

The Eleusian and Bacchic Mysteries, by Thomas Taylor: Wizards Bookshelf, San Diego 1980.

Origins, A Short Etymological Dictionary of Modern English, by Eric Partridge: Macmillan Co., NY 1959.

The Search For Ancient Egypt, by Jean Vercoutter: Thames & Hudson, NY 1992.

The Egyptians, by Cyril Aldred: Thames & Hudson Inc., 1988.

The Holy Bible Revised Standard Edition: Thomas Nelson & Sons, NY 1953.

Encyclopaedia Britannica, 1943 edition.

New Encyclopaedia Britannica-Micropaedia, 1981 edition.

Myth and Law Among the Indo-Europeans, ed. by Jaan Puhvel, Berkeley
    & Los Angeles, 1970.

Encyclopedia of Religion and Ethics, by L.H. Gray, ed. by James Hastings.

Herodotus the Histories, trans. By Aubrey de Selincourt, Penguin Books
    1979.

The Ramayana Told by Aubrey Menen: Charles scribner's Sons, NY 1954.

The Religions of Man by Huston Smith: Harper & Row, NY 1958.

Printed in the United States
by Baker & Taylor Publisher Services